THE TRUTH ABOUT
EARLY AMERICAN HISTORY

# THE TRUTH ABOUT
# COLONIAL HISTORY

CHARLOTTE TAYLOR

Enslow
PUBLISHING

Please visit our website, www.enslow.com. For a free color catalog of all our high-quality books, call toll free 1-800-398-2504 or fax 1-877-980-4454.

**Cataloging-in-Publication Data**

Names: Taylor, Charlotte, 1978-.
Title: The truth about colonial history / Charlotte Taylor.
Description: New York : Enslow Publishing, 2023. | Series: The truth about early American history | Includes glossary and index.
Identifiers: ISBN 9781978527782 (pbk.) | ISBN 9781978527805 (library bound) | ISBN 9781978527799 (6pack) | ISBN 9781978527812 (ebook)
Subjects: LCSH: United States–History–Colonial period, ca. 1600-1775–Juvenile literature.
Classification: LCC E188.T39 2023 | DDC 973.3–dc23

Published in 2023 by
**Enslow Publishing**
29 E. 21st Street
New York, NY 10010

Portions of this work were originally authored by Julia McDonnell and published as *The Pilgrims Didn't Celebrate the First Thanksgiving: Exposing Myths About Colonial History*. All new material in this edition was authored by Charlotte Taylor.

Designer: Rachel Rising
Editor: Megan Quick

Photo credits: Cover, p. 20 Everett Collection/Shutterstock.com; Cover, pp. 1-4, 6-8, 10-12, 14, 16-18, 20- 22, 24, 26, 28, 30-32 pashabo/Shutterstock.com; Cover, pp. 1-4, 6-8, 10-12, 14, 16-18, 20- 22, 24, 26, 28, 30-32 orangeberry/Shutterstock.com; Cover, pp. pp. 1-4, 6-8, 10-12, 14, 16-18, 20- 22, 24, 26, 28, 30-32 iulias/Shutterstock.com; Cover Brian A Jackson/Shutterstock.com; Cover, pp. 1, 3, 4, 7, 8, 11, 12, 14, 17, 18, 21, 22, 24, 26, 28, 30-32 Epifantsev/Shutterstock.com; p. 5 I. Pilon/Shutterstock.com; p. 6 Gift of Edgar William and Bernice Chrysler Garbisch; p. 7 https://en.wikipedia.org/wiki/File:Portrait_of_a_Man,_Said_to_be_Christopher_Columbus.jpg; p. 9 Sean Pavone/Shutterstock.com; p. 10 https://en.wikipedia.org/wiki/File:Pocahontas-saves-Smith-NE-Chromo-1870.jpeg#/media/File:Pocahontas-saves-Smith-NE-Chromo-1870.jpeg; p. 11 https://en.wikipedia.org/wiki/Pocahontas#/media/File:Baptism_of_Pocahontas.jpg; p. 13 https://en.wikipedia.org/wiki/Mayflower#/media/File:Copyrighted_and_Published_by_A_S_Burbank,_The_Mayflower_at_Sea_(NBY_21340).jpg; p. 15 vagabond54/Shutterstock.com; p. 16 Logan Bush/Shutterstock.com; p. 17 https://commons.wikimedia.org/wiki/File:Thanksgiving-Brownscombe.jpg; p. 19 https://commons.wikimedia.org/wiki/File:Green_Corn_Ceremony_-_Minatarrees.jpg; p. 21 https://en.wikipedia.org/wiki/File:HouseWhereWitchcraftStarted.png#/media/File:HouseWhereWitchcraftStarted.png; p. 23 https://en.wikipedia.org/wiki/File:SlaveDanceand_Music.jpg; p. 25 https://commons.wikimedia.org/wiki/File:Slavery_in_the_13_colonies.jpg; p. 27 https://commons.wikimedia.org/wiki/File:Indians_ambush_British_at_Battle_of_the_Monongahela.jpg; p. 29 https://commons.wikimedia.org/wiki/File:The_Battle_of_Lexington.jpg.

Printed in the United States of America

CPSIA compliance information: Batch #CSENS23: For further information contact Enslow Publishing, New York, New York, at 1-800-398-2504.

Find us on 🅕 🅞

# CONTENTS

FACT OR FAIRY TALE? .......................... 4

COLUMBUS MISSES THE MARK ............... 6

EARLY ARRIVALS................................. 8

NOT A LOVE STORY ........................... 10

A ROUGH RIDE................................. 12

AMERICA'S MOST FAMOUS ROCK ............ 14

PARTY WITH THE PILGRIMS.................. 16

NOT THE FIRST TIME ........................ 18

HUNTING FOR WITCHES ..................... 20

ENSLAVED PEOPLE IN THE COLONIES ..... 22

SLAVERY IN THE NORTH ..................... 24

COMING OUT FIGHTING ...................... 26

UNCOVERING THE TRUTH ................... 28

GLOSSARY .................................... 30

FOR MORE INFORMATION .................. 31

INDEX........................................ 32

WORDS IN THE GLOSSARY APPEAR IN **BOLD** TYPE
THE FIRST TIME THEY ARE USED IN THE TEXT.

# FACT OR FAIRY TALE?

Some of the most interesting facts about the history of colonial America are about what did not happen: Christopher Columbus did not discover North America. The Pilgrims did not invite the Native Americans to the first Thanksgiving feast. The *Mayflower* was not built to carry passengers.

You have probably heard many stories about America's early years. But sometimes what we learn is not the whole truth. Over time, stories change and facts get confused. Learning real stories about the past is a great way to understand the true history of colonial America.

## EXPLORE MORE!

MOST OF THE ORIGINAL 13 COLONIES WERE NAMED AFTER BRITISH PEOPLE OR PLACES. MASSACHUSETTS WAS THE ONLY COLONY NAMED AFTER A NATIVE TRIBE. CONNECTICUT'S NAME CAME FROM AN ALGONQUIAN WORD THAT ROUGHLY MEANS "LAND ON THE LONG TIDAL RIVER."

A colony is an area that is controlled by another country, which is usually far away. England was about 3,000 miles (4,830 km) from the American colonies.

A Map of the
UNITED STATES
OF
AMERICA,
with Part of the
ADJOINING PROVINCES
from the latest Authorities.

**5**

British Statute Miles.

# COLUMBUS MISSES THE MARK

Christopher Columbus was an Italian **explorer**. His most famous voyages were for Spain. But the claim that he discovered North America on these voyages is false.

Columbus was trying to find a way to sail west from Europe to Asia. He did not succeed.

In 1492, millions of Native People were already living on the North American continent. Vikings from Greenland were the first Europeans known to have set foot in North America. They landed around the year 1000.

Even though Columbus did not discover North America, his travels opened up a whole new area that Europeans wanted to explore and colonize. This marked the beginning of the colonial period.

CHRISTOPHER COLUMBUS

## EXPLORE MORE!

COLUMBUS PROBABLY FIRST LANDED ON THE ISLAND THAT HE NAMED SAN SALVADOR. THIS IS PART OF THE CHAIN OF ISLANDS NOW KNOWN AS THE BAHAMAS. COLUMBUS BELIEVED HE HAD REACHED SOUTHEAST ASIA. ON HIS THREE OTHER VOYAGES, HE EXPLORED OTHER AREAS IN THE CARIBBEAN AS WELL AS THE COASTS OF CENTRAL AND SOUTH AMERICA.

# EARLY ARRIVALS

In 1565, a Spanish explorer planted his country's flag on the east coast of Florida. The area would become Saint Augustine, Florida—the first European settlement in North America. It was another 55 years before the Pilgrims settled in Plymouth, Massachusetts, in 1620.

Many people think of Plymouth as the original colony of North America. But there were several successful colonies before the Pilgrims arrived. In addition to the Spanish in Saint Augustine, the Dutch settled in New Netherland (now New York and other areas) about 1614. Before that, the British founded Jamestown in Virginia in 1607.

## EXPLORE MORE!

MANY EUROPEANS SETTLED IN NORTH AMERICA LONG BEFORE JAMESTOWN AND PLYMOUTH WERE FOUNDED. HOWEVER, THEIR COLONIES DID NOT LAST. ONE OF THESE WAS THE "LOST COLONY" OF ROANOKE, FOUNDED IN 1587. ALL OF THE SETTLERS DISAPPEARED. WHAT HAPPENED TO THEM IS STILL A MYSTERY.

You can still see signs of the Spanish history of Saint Augustine, Florida, throughout the city and its buildings.

# NOT A LOVE STORY

Pocahontas was the young daughter of Chief Powhatan, the leader of the Powhatan peoples living near Jamestown, Virginia. John Smith was a British soldier from the settlement. In 1607, the chief's brother captured Smith. Much later, Smith claimed that Pocahontas saved him from being killed by the Powhatans.

There are stories about Smith and Pocahontas being in love. This isn't true. She would have been young, only about 11, at the time. She may have saved Smith's life, or he may have been part of a Powhatan **ceremony** that he didn't understand. However, Pocahontas later visited Jamestown. She and Smith may have taught each other words in their languages.

After Pocahontas was captured by the British, she became a Christian. She was given the English name Rebecca.

## EXPLORE MORE!

POCAHONTAS MAY HAVE HAD TWO HUSBANDS IN HER LIFETIME. STORIES SAY THE FIRST WAS KOCOUM, A **WARRIOR** WHO MAY HAVE BEEN FROM ANOTHER TRIBE. IN 1613, WHEN THE ENGLISH CAPTURED POCAHONTAS AND SHE WAS A PRISONER, SHE MET A PLANTER NAMED JOHN ROLFE. THEY MARRIED AND LATER TRAVELED TO ENGLAND.

# A ROUGH RIDE

The *Mayflower* did not usually carry passengers—it was a **cargo** ship. It was probably only about 90 feet (27.4 m) long. There were 102 passengers on board when it set sail in September 1620. The ship was cold, wet, and overcrowded. Illnesses spread, and lack of good food weakened the passengers.

All of the *Mayflower's* passengers are considered Pilgrims, but only about a third were Puritans. In fact, they were part of a group within the Puritans called Separatists. They wanted to split from the Church of England. They wanted a new place to practice their **religion**. The other passengers were seeking adventure or wealth.

## EXPLORE MORE!

THE *MAYFLOWER* WAS NOT SUPPOSED TO MAKE THE JOURNEY ACROSS THE ATLANTIC ALONE. A SMALL SHIP CALLED THE *SPEEDWELL* STARTED OFF WITH THE *MAYFLOWER*. BUT THE *SPEEDWELL* LEAKED BADLY. AFTER TWO FAILED ATTEMPTS AT SAILING, THE TRAVELERS HAD TO LEAVE THE SHIP IN ENGLAND.

After the *Mayflower* reached Plymouth in December, the passengers lived on board until the spring. Only half survived that winter.

13

# AMERICA'S MOST FAMOUS ROCK

When the *Mayflower* arrived in North America, its first stop was not Plymouth. The Pilgrims first left the ship at what is now Cape Cod, Massachusetts. A few weeks later, they traveled on to Plymouth. And no one who was there said anything about a rock when leaving the ship.

About 120 years later, a colonist's son reported he'd been told a rock in Plymouth Harbor was the Pilgrim's landing spot. Even though there was no proof, the story took hold. Plymouth Rock became a **symbol** of the settlers' struggles.

## EXPLORE MORE!

IN 1774, TOWNSPEOPLE TRIED TO MOVE PLYMOUTH ROCK. IT SPLIT IN TWO. YEARS LATER, THE ROCK WAS DROPPED AND BROKEN AGAIN. IT WAS FINALLY PUT BACK TOGETHER IN 1880. PIECES OF THE ROCK HAVE BEEN CHIPPED AWAY OVER THE YEARS. SOME PEOPLE ARE SURPRISED AT HOW SMALL THE ROCK IS NOW!

Plymouth Rock weighs about 10 tons (9.1 mt) today, but in 1620 it may have weighed from 40 to 200 tons (36.3 to 181.4 mt).

15

# PARTY WITH THE PILGRIMS

The Pilgrims' first **harvest** gathering was not really a thanksgiving event. Usually when Puritans gave thanks, they **fasted** and prayed. The feast in 1621 was a party. The settlers were celebrating their first successful harvest.

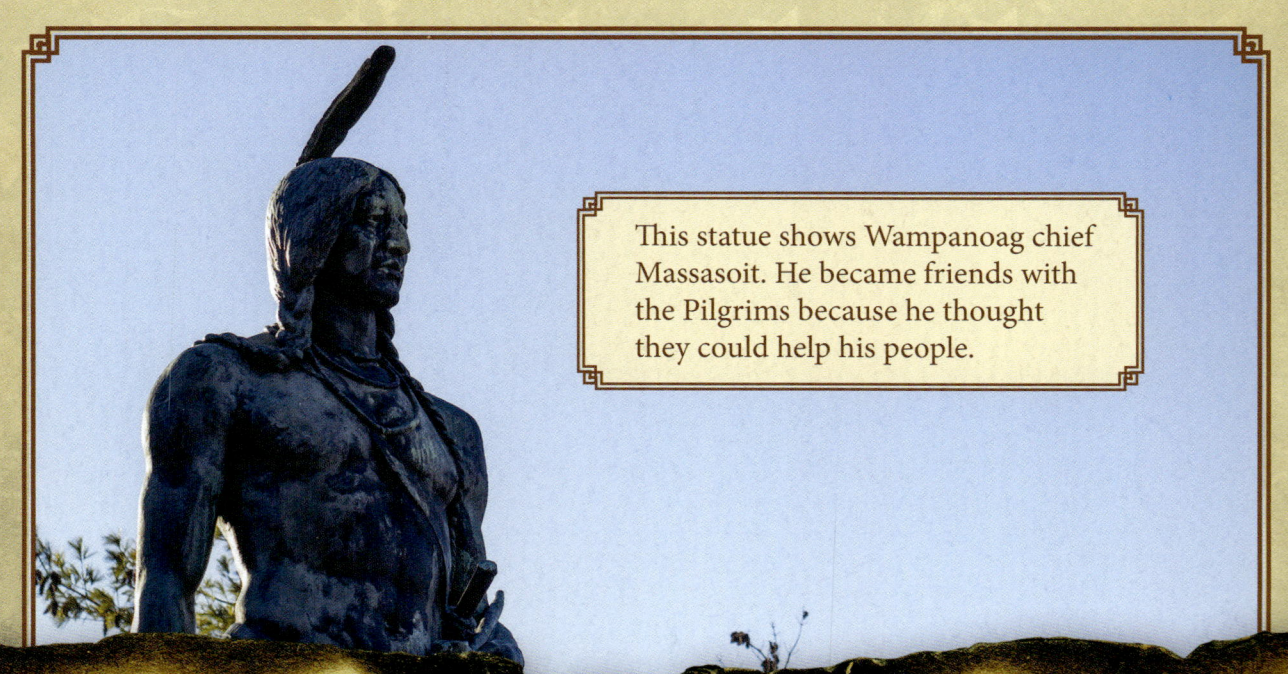

This statue shows Wampanoag chief Massasoit. He became friends with the Pilgrims because he thought they could help his people.

The Wampanoag people had taught them how to plant corn, beans, and squash.

Despite the Wampanoags' help, they were not invited to the three-day feast. Some think the Wampanoags heard guns fired in celebration or in a hunt. Wampanoag chief Massasoit and 90 of his men arrived to see if there was trouble—and stayed to eat!

# EXPLORE MORE!

THE PILGRIMS AND WAMPANOAGS MAY HAVE EATEN TURKEY AT THE FEAST, BUT THEY MORE LIKELY ATE GOOSE OR DUCK. THEY PROBABLY ALSO ENJOYED DEER, SHELLFISH, AND EEL ALONG WITH CORN AND SQUASH. PROBABLY NOT ON THE MENU? POTATOES AND PUMPKIN PIE.

# NOT THE FIRST TIME

The 1621 thanksgiving feast wasn't really the first in North America. Each autumn, many Native American peoples gathered to give thanks for the harvest. And European explorers before the Pilgrims held celebrations too.

The Spanish held thanksgiving events in Texas in 1541 and 1598. In 1607, members of the Abenaki Tribe and British settlers in Maine shared a harvest feast. It wasn't until the 1890s that the idea of the Pilgrims and Native Americans feasting together in 1621 became important to the Thanksgiving story.

## EXPLORE MORE!

NATIVE AMERICANS—BOTH THEN AND NOW— HAVE THEIR OWN THANKSGIVING **TRADITIONS**. SOME TRIBES IN THE SOUTHEASTERN UNITED STATES STILL CELEBRATE THE GREEN CORN CEREMONY. IN LATE SUMMER OR EARLY FALL, TRIBE MEMBERS GIVE THANKS FOR THE CORN HARVEST THROUGH DANCE, FEASTS, FASTING, AND RELIGIOUS CEREMONIES.

A group of men give thanks for the harvest at a Green Corn ceremony.

# HUNTING FOR WITCHES

Witch hunts in the colonies began almost 50 years before the famous witch trials in Salem, Massachusetts. In 1647, a woman named Alse Young was found guilty of being a witch. She was then hanged in Hartford, Connecticut. Young was the first person in the colony to be killed after charges of witchcraft, but she was not the last.

This drawing shows a scene from the Salem witch trials. They were the most famous American witch trials but not the first.

When eight-year-old Elizabeth Kelly of Hartford became sick and died in 1662, her parents wanted answers. They blamed a neighbor. Soon, many neighbors were accusing each other of witchcraft. Four were hanged. By 1697, more than 40 people in Connecticut had been charged with witchcraft.

The Salem witch hunts began in this home in Danvers, Massachusetts.

# EXPLORE MORE!

THE SALEM WITCH TRIALS HAPPENED IN 1692 AND 1693. THE WITCH HUNTS BEGAN WHEN SEVERAL GIRLS CLAIMED THE DEVIL HAD POSSESSED THEM, OR TAKEN THEM OVER. THEY SAID SEVERAL WOMEN IN TOWN WERE WITCHES. WITHIN MONTHS, MORE THAN 150 PEOPLE HAD BEEN ACCUSED OF WITCHCRAFT. ABOUT 20 WERE KILLED, WHILE MORE DIED IN JAIL.

# ENSLAVED PEOPLE IN THE COLONIES

Many history books teach that the first Africans were brought to North America in 1619. However, Europeans were bringing enslaved people to the Americas as early as the 1400s. Most were African, but enslavers also captured Native Americans or bought them from other tribes that held them as prisoners.

In 1808, it became unlawful to bring enslaved people to the United States. However, a child born to a mother who was enslaved was considered to be enslaved too. This meant that slavery continued in North America for many more decades.

## EXPLORE MORE!

MOST ENSLAVERS TOOK ENSLAVED PEOPLE FROM THE CENTRAL WEST COAST OF AFRICA. SHIPS TOOK THEM TO SOUTH, CENTRAL, OR NORTH AMERICA. THE LONG TRIP ACROSS THE ATLANTIC OCEAN, KNOWN AS THE MIDDLE PASSAGE, COULD BE DEADLY. ABOUT 15 PERCENT OF ENSLAVED PEOPLE DIED BEFORE REACHING THE AMERICAS.

Many Africans, like those pictured here, were taken from their homes and enslaved in the American colonies. Native Americans were also forced into slavery.

23

# SLAVERY IN THE NORTH

Slavery was a central part of life in the southern United States for many years. However, the idea that slavery was only in the South is untrue. All 13 original colonies allowed slavery. At one point, northern colonists owned more than 40,000 enslaved people. And by 1740, enslaved people made up about 20 percent of New York City's population.

In the North, many enslaved people lived in cities, working as laborers and servants. Enslaved women often did household jobs, while men did physical work. In the South, many enslaved people worked in the fields of large farms called plantations.

## EXPLORE MORE!

MANY OF AMERICA'S FOUNDING FATHERS—INCLUDING LEADERS FROM BOTH THE NORTH AND THE SOUTH— TOOK PART IN SLAVERY. GEORGE WASHINGTON AND BEN FRANKLIN BOTH OWNED ENSLAVED PEOPLE. EVEN SOME OF THE PEOPLE WHO SPOKE OUT AGAINST SLAVERY, SUCH AS THOMAS JEFFERSON, WERE ENSLAVERS.

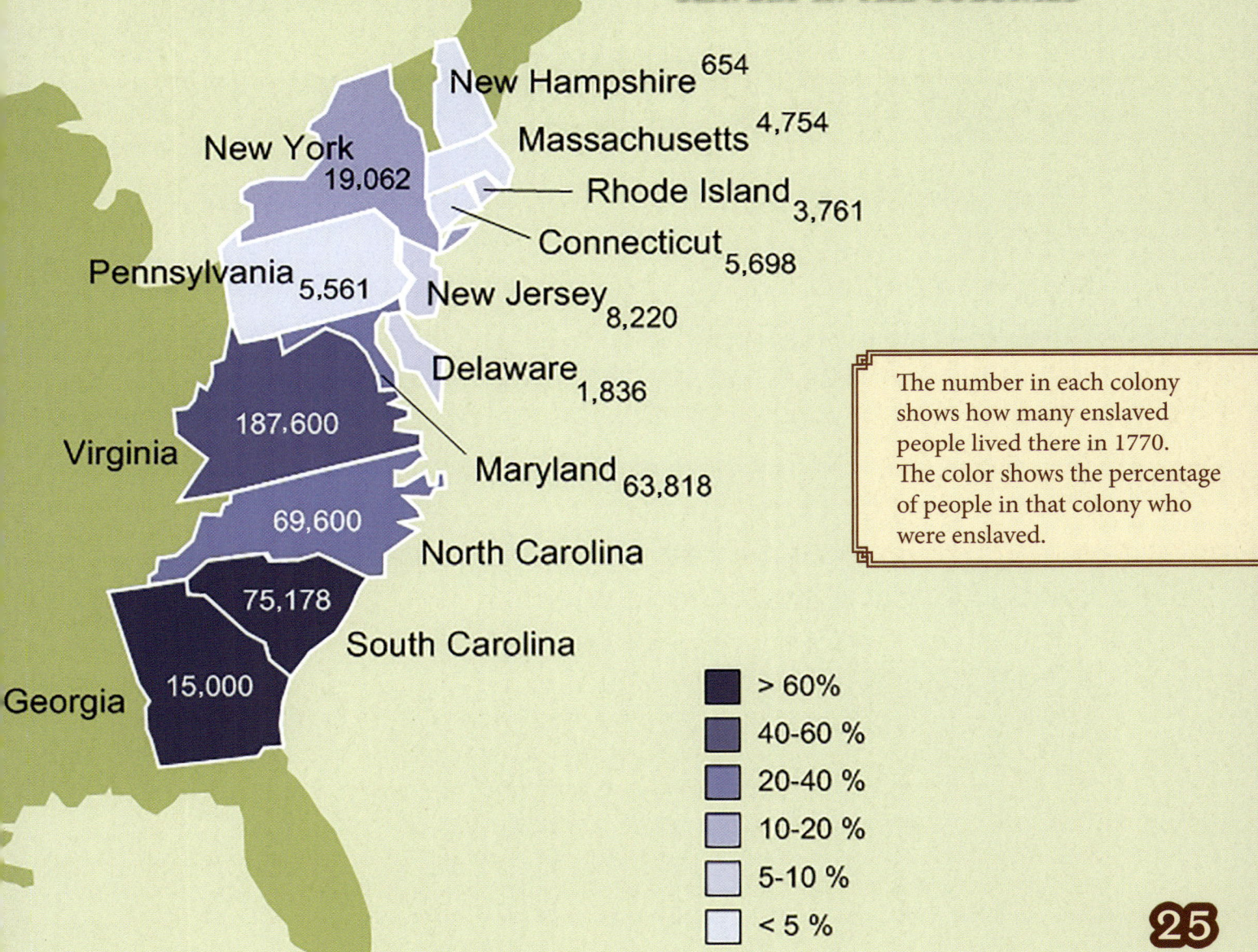

# SLAVERY IN THE COLONIES

New Hampshire 654
Massachusetts 4,754
Rhode Island 3,761
Connecticut 5,698
New York 19,062
New Jersey 8,220
Pennsylvania 5,561
Delaware 1,836
Virginia 187,600
Maryland 63,818
North Carolina 69,600
South Carolina 75,178
Georgia 15,000

The number in each colony shows how many enslaved people lived there in 1770. The color shows the percentage of people in that colony who were enslaved.

> 60%
40-60 %
20-40 %
10-20 %
5-10 %
< 5 %

25

# COMING OUT FIGHTING

When we think of colonists at war, the American Revolution (1775–1783) probably comes to mind. However, there were many other **conflicts** involving the colonists. Many of these were against Native American nations. The colonists thought they should have the Native Americans' land.

Other conflicts occurred between England, Spain, France, the Netherlands, and their colonies in the Americas. Some of these wars were part of larger European wars. Other conflicts began over territory. Each country wanted a larger piece of the land that would become the United States.

## EXPLORE MORE!

NATIVE AMERICAN GROUPS AND THE COLONISTS OFTEN FOUGHT EACH OTHER. HOWEVER, WHEN THEY HAD COMMON ENEMIES, SOME NATIVE PEOPLES CHOSE TO FIGHT ALONGSIDE THE COLONISTS. THE BRITISH COLONISTS MIGHT NOT HAVE WON THE FRENCH AND INDIAN WAR (1754—1763) WITHOUT THE HELP OF NATIVE AMERICAN ALLIES—ALTHOUGH THE FRENCH ALSO HAD HELP FROM OTHER NATIVE AMERICAN GROUPS.

The French and Indian War started over whether Great Britain or France had the right to certain land in North America. Different Native American tribes fought with each side.

27

# UNCOVERING THE TRUTH

American history is full of stories. The people who passed those stories on may have changed them over the years—either by accident or on purpose. Maybe they wanted to make a story more interesting. Or maybe they wanted to make people feel better about an event.

America has a rich and **complicated** history. We study history so that we can learn from it. That's why it's important to find out the truth about the past. You can do this by asking questions and reading a lot. You might be surprised at what you find out!

## EXPLORE MORE!

BY THE MIDDLE OF THE 1700S, MANY COLONISTS WERE UNHAPPY WITH BRITISH RULE. GREAT BRITAIN PASSED LAWS AND TAXES THAT THE COLONISTS THOUGHT WERE UNFAIR. THE COLONISTS DECLARED THEIR INDEPENDENCE FROM GREAT BRITAIN IN 1776.

The Battles of Lexington and Concord on April 19, 1775, marked the start of the American Revolution and the colonies' fight to be free from the British.

# GLOSSARY

**cargo:** Having to do with goods carried by a ship, train, or truck.

**ceremony:** An event to honor or celebrate something.

**complicated:** Hard to understand, explain, or deal with.

**conflict:** A struggle for power or property.

**explorer:** A person who travels to a place in order to learn more about it.

**fast:** To eat no food for a period of time.

**harvest**: Having to do with crops that are gathered.

**religion:** A belief in and way of honoring a god or gods.

**symbol:** A picture, shape, or object that stands for something else.

**tradition:** A long-practiced custom.

**warrior:** A soldier.

# FOR MORE INFORMATION

## BOOKS

Raum, Elizabeth. *The Scoop on Clothes, Homes, and Daily Life in Colonial America*. North Mankato, MN: Capstone Press, 2017.

Romero, Libby. *The Mayflower*. New York, NY: DK, 2020.

Rusick, Jessica. *Living in the Jamestown Colony: A This or That Debate*. North Mankato, MN: Capstone Press, 2020

## WEBSITES

**Ducksters: Colonial America for Kids**
*www.ducksters.com/history/colonial_america/*
Learn more about important people, events, and daily life in colonial America.

**Salem Witch Museum: Kids' Questions**
*salemwitchmuseum.com/video-categories/kids-questions/*
Check out the fascinating answers to kids' questions about the witch hunts.

**Scholastic: The First Thanksgiving**
*www.scholastic.com/scholastic_thanksgiving/webcast.htm*
This site includes videos about the *Mayflower* as well as the daily lives of the Pilgrims and Wampanoags.

# INDEX

Africa, 22, 23

American Revolution, 26, 29

Columbus, Christopher, 4, 6, 7

England, 5, 11, 12

Founding Fathers, 24

French and Indian War, 26, 27

Hartford, Connecticut, 20, 21

harvest, 16, 18, 19

Jamestown, 8, 10, 11

*Mayflower*, 4, 12, 13, 14

Massasoit, 16, 17

Native Americans, 4, 7, 18, 22, 23, 26, 27

Pilgrims, 4, 8, 12, 16, 17, 18

Plymouth, 8, 14

Plymouth Rock, 14, 15

Pocahontas, 10, 11

Powhatan, 10, 11

Puritans, 12, 16

Roanoke, 8

Saint Augustine, 8, 9

Salem, Massachusetts, 20, 21

slavery, 22, 23, 24, 25

Smith, John, 10, 11

Thanksgiving, 4, 16, 17, 18

13 colonies, 4, 5, 24

Wampanoag, 16, 17

witch hunts/trials, 20, 21